DATE DUE

Earthforms

Archipelagoes

by Xavier Niz

Consultant:
John D. Vitek
Professor of Geology

**Lincoln School
Library Media Center
Mundelein, IL**

Capstone press

Mankato, Minnesota

Bridgestone Books are published by Capstone Press,
151 Good Counsel Drive, P.O. Box 669, Mankato, Minnesota 56002.
www.capstonepress.com

Library of Congress Cataloging-in-Publication Data
Niz, Xavier.
    Archipelagoes / Xavier Niz.
        p. cm.—(Bridgestone books. Earthforms)
    Summary: "Describes archipelagoes, including how they form, plants and animals on archipelagoes,
how people and weather change archipelagoes, archipelagoes in North America, and the
Malay Archipelago"—Provided by publisher.
    Includes bibliographical references and index.
    ISBN 0-7368-4306-X (hardcover)
    1. Archipelagoes—Juvenile literature. I. Title. II. Series.
GB471.N59 2006
551.42—dc22   2004028514

Editorial Credits

Becky Viaene, editor; Juliette Peters, set designer; Kate Opseth, book designer; Anne P. McMullen,
    illustrator; Wanda Winch, photo researcher; Scott Thoms, photo editor

Photo Credits

Art Directors/Mark Both, 18
Bruce Coleman Inc./James Blank, 14; Kenneth W. Fink, 16
Corbis/Bonnie B. Pelnar, cover; Macduff Everton, 1; Richard Hamilton Smith, 12
Minden Pictures/Frans Lanting, 8
Tom Stack & Associates, Inc./Ed Robinson, 4; Mark Allan Stack, 10

1 2 3 4 5 6 10 09 08 07 06 05

Table of Contents

What Are Archipelagoes?

Archipelagoes are chains of islands. Archipelago means "chief sea." The word first was used to describe the Aegean Sea. Later, it meant islands in the Aegean Sea. Today, the word archipelago describes any chain of islands.

Archipelagoes vary in size. Some have just a few islands. Others, such as the Malay Archipelago, contain thousands of islands.

◄ An archipelago of about 100 Pacific Ocean islands form the nation of Palau, or Belau.

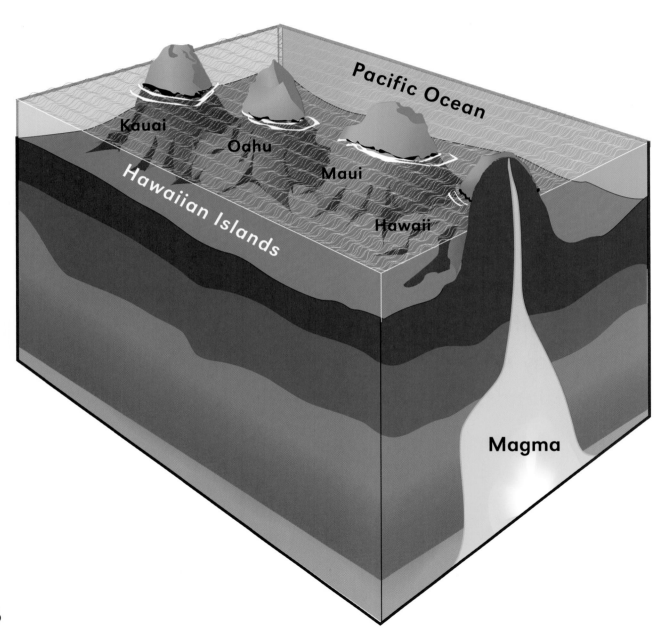

Pacific Ocean

Kauai

Oahu

Maui

Hawaii

Hawaiian Islands

Magma

How Do Archipelagoes Form?

Underwater **volcanoes** form many archipelagoes. As rising magma reaches the ocean floor, it is called **lava**. Lava cools and forms piles on the ocean floor. Piles that rise above ocean water are islands.

Archipelagoes are also formed by rising water levels. Rising water can cover low land on peninsulas. Higher lands that stay above water become islands off the **mainland**.

Tiny sea **corals** also form archipelagoes. Many coral skeletons pile up to form islands.

◄ Rising magma became lava when it reached the ocean floor and formed this part of the Hawaiian Islands.

Plants on Archipelagoes

At first, no plants grow on archipelagoes formed by volcanoes. Later, wind, water, birds, and people carry seeds to the land. People brought the first pineapple plants to the Hawaiian Islands. Many of these plants still grow on the islands.

Climate affects which plants grow on an archipelago. The Hawaiian Islands are hot and wet. Silversword plants are found only on these islands. Short grasses grow on Canada's cold Arctic Archipelago.

◄ Silversword plants' color helps them reflect sunlight and avoid burning in the hot Hawaiian climate.

Animals on Archipelagoes

Most archipelagoes had no animals living on them when they formed. Animals later **migrated** to islands from nearby land. Great blue herons live near Canada's coast on the Queen Charlotte Islands. During long trips, these birds rest on other archipelagoes.

Animals that don't fly can float or swim to islands. Anolis lizards got to the Caribbean Archipelago from South America by floating or swimming. Snakes and rats float to islands on broken tree branches.

◀ A great blue heron sits still, waiting to catch a fish. The bird flies to islands in a group, but it hunts alone.

Weather Changes Archipelagoes

Wind and waves can add islands to an archipelago. Strong storms push sand from islands into the ocean. Over time, moving sand can split one island into two.

Wind and waves can also cause archipelagoes to disappear. Low-lying islands can be completely flooded by storms. Wind and waves can slowly **erode** islands until nothing is left above water.

◄ Stormy weather pushes powerful waves into land. Over time, crashing waves will change the land's shape.

People Change Archipelagoes

People can cause big changes to islands in an archipelago. People clear land to build houses and hotels. They connect islands with roads. The Overseas Highway connects the islands of the Florida Keys to Florida.

People also affect islands' plants and animals. They bring new plants and animals to islands. New animals can destroy **native** plants and animals. People brought cats and dogs to Hawaii. These animals killed many native Hawaiian birds.

◄ Many people cross the Florida Keys on the 128-mile-long (206-kilometer-long) Overseas Highway.

Archipelagoes in North America

One of the world's longest chain of small islands is in Alaska. About 150 islands make up Alaska's Aleutian Islands. The islands spread across 1,200 miles (1,930 kilometers).

Fifty large islands make up Canada's Arctic Archipelago. They cover more land than any other archipelago in North America. These islands stretch from Alaska to Greenland. The Arctic Archipelago covers more than 550,000 square miles (1.4 million square kilometers).

◄ Terrible Mountain rises from Attu Island. Attu Island is one of the Aleutian Islands.

Malay Archipelago

The Malay Archipelago is the largest archipelago in the world. It covers almost 1.1 million square miles (2.8 million square kilometers).

Thousands of islands make up the Malay Archipelago. It includes the countries of Indonesia, Papua New Guinea, the Philippines, and Brunei. It also includes the Malaysian states Sarawak and Sabah.

◄ Located in Papua New Guinea's Morobe Province, this tiny village is one of many in the Malay Archipelago.

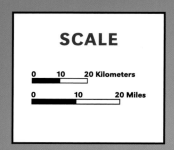

N

W ⊙ E

S

F L O R I D A

Gulf of Mexico

Florida Bay

F L O R I D A   K E Y S

Key Largo

Islamorada

Long Key

Marathon

Atlantic Ocean

Key West

Big Pine and The Lower Keys

Archipelagoes on a Map

Archipelagoes are easy to find on a map. Look for pieces of land surrounded by water. Then look to see if these islands form a chain.

Archipelagoes are constantly changing. The sizes and shapes of archipelagoes may change each year. Volcanoes, water levels, and coral form new archipelagoes. Wind and waves create or erode islands in an archipelago. Maps of archipelagoes will continue to be updated.

◀ Many islands make up the archipelago known as the Florida Keys.

Glossary

climate (KLYE-mit)—the usual weather in a place

coral (KOR-uhl)—an underwater substance made up of the skeletons of tiny sea creatures

erode (i-RODE)—to wear away; wind and water erode soil and rock.

lava (LAH-vuh)—the hot, liquid rock that pours out of a volcano when it erupts

mainland (MAYN-luhnd)—the largest land mass of a country, territory, or continent, as opposed to its islands or peninsulas

migrate (MYE-grate)—to move from one place to another when seasons change or when food is scarce

native (NAY-tiv)—a person, an animal, or a plant that originally lived or grew in a certain place

volcano (vol-KAY-noh)—an underground vent that lava, ash, and gas erupt out of; most volcanoes are tall and cone-shaped.

Read More

Royston, Angela. *Islands.* My World of Geography. Chicago: Heinemann Library, 2005.

Webster, Christine. *Islands.* Earthforms. Mankato, Minn.: Capstone Press, 2005.

Internet Sites

FactHound offers a safe, fun way to find Internet sites related to this book. All of the sites on FactHound have been researched by our staff.

Here's how:
1. Visit *www.facthound.com*
2. Type in this special code **073684306X** for age-appropriate sites. Or enter a search word related to this book for a more general search.
3. Click on the **Fetch It** button.

FactHound will fetch the best sites for you!

Index